THE PICTORIAL SYMBOLS
OF ALCHEMY

ARTHUR EDWARD WAITE

The Hermetic Mystery - upon the higher interpretation of which I have spoken at considerable length in the previous paper and have created an analogy between its hidden meaning and that which I should term the centre of the Religions Mystery in Christendom- is the only branch of mystic and occult literature which lent itself to the decorative sense. I suppose that there are few people comparatively who at this day have any notion of the extent to which that sense was developed in the books of the adepts. It will be understood that in speaking now upon this subject I am leaving my proper path, but though the fact does not seem to have been registered, it is so utterly curious to note how a literature which is most dark and inscrutable of all has at the same time its lighter side- a side, indeed, of pleasant inventions, of apologue, of parable, of explicit enigma, above all of poetry. The fact is that alchemy presented itself as an art, its books were the work of artists; and for the sym-pathetic reader, even when he may understand them least, they will read sometimes like enchanting fables or legends. When in this manner some of the writers had exhausted their resources in language, they had recourse to illustrations, and I wonder almost that no one has thought to collect the amazing copper-plates which literally did adorn the Latin and other tracts of the seventeenth century. As I propose to print some selected specimens of the pictorial art in alchemy because they are exceedingly curious, and not for a deeper reason, the reader will not expect, and for once in a way will perhaps be rather relieved, that I am not going in quest especially of their inner meanings. So far as may be possible, the pictures shall speak for themselves, seeing that I write for the moment rather as a lover of books- a bibliophile- than a lover of learning. I will begin, however, with a definition. The alchemists whom I have in my mind may be classified as artists on the decorative side and in their illustrations- but I know not whether they were their own draughtsmen- they approached the Rabelaisian method. The school on both sides is rather of Germanic origin; and it is such entirely, so far as the pictures are concerned. The French alchemists had recourse occasionally to designs, but they are negligible for the present purpose. This is a clearance of the ground, but it must be added that the great and authoritative text-books have not been illustrated- as, for example, *The Open Entrance to the Closed Palace o/ the King*, which is the work of Eirenaeus Philalethes, and the *New Light o/ Alchemy*, which is. believed to be that of. Alexander Seton. If I may attempt such a comparison, Philalethes- in the work mentioned- reads rather like a Pauline epistle and Seton like an *Epistle to the Hebrews* but the. analogy in both cases is intended to be allusive only, and strict in no sense. So also they read here and there as if they were almost inspired; but they could not be termed decorative. The really

4

practical works- as, for example, the Latin treatises ascribed to Geber- are never illustrated, except by crude sketches of material vessels used in the material art for the aid of the neophyte on his way to the transmutation of metals. I do not think that they really helped him, and they are of no account for our purpose. The pictures of the adepts were the allegorical properties of the adepts, and though the criticism has a side of harshness they were almost obviously provided for the further confusion of the inquirer, under the pretence of his enlightenment. At the same time, authors or artists were sages after their own manner, their allegories had a set purpose and represent throughout a prevailing school of symbolism. It is quite easy to work out the elementary part of the symbolism; it is not difficult to speculate reasonably about some of the more obscure materials. But the true canons of alchemical criticism yet remain to be expounded; and I believe that I have intimated otherwise the difficulty and urgency attaching to this work, so that there may be one unerring criterion to distinguish between the texts representing the spiritual and those of the physical work. On the latter phase of the subject it would be useless- and more than useless- to discourse in any periodical, even if I. could claim to care anything and to know sufficiently thereof. I know neither enough to hold my tongue nor enough to speak, so that I differ in this respect- but for once only- from my . excellent precursor Elias Ashmole. Like him and like Thomas Vaughan, I do know the narrowness of the name *Chemia,* with the antiquity and infinity of the proper object of research; thereon we have all borne true witness in our several days and generations. It is a matter of common report that the old Hermetic adepts were the chemists of their time and that, as such, they made numerous and valuable discoveries. This is true in a general sense, but under what is also a general and an exceedingly grave reserve. There is little need to say in the first place, that the spiritual alchemists made no researches and could have had no findings in the world of metals and minerals. Secondly, there was a great concourse of witnesses in secret literature, who were adepts of neither branch; but they expressed their dreams and speculations in terms of spurious certitude, and were often sincere in the sense that they deceived themselves. They produced sophistications in the physical work and believed that their tinctures and colorations were the work of philosophy; these discovered nothing, and misled nearly every one. They also- in the alternative school- pursued erroneous ways or translated their aspirations at a distance into root-matter of spiritual Hermetic tradition; they reached the term of their folly and drew others who were foolish after them, who had also no law of differentiation between things of Caesar and God. Finally- but of these I say nothing- there were arrant impostors, representing the colportage of their time, who trafficked in the interest of the curious, assuming alchemy for their province, as others of the secret sciences were exploited by others of their kindred. Now, between all these the official historians of chemistry in the near past had no ground of distinction, and there is little certainty that they were right over many or most of their judgments. Once more, the canon was wanting; as I have shown that in another region it is either wanting for ourselves, or- to be correct- is in course only of development. This work, therefore, was largely one of divination, with a peculiar uncertainty in the results. I have now finished with this introductory part, and I offer in the first place a simple illustration of the alchemist's laboratory, as it was conceived by Michael Maier at the beginning of the seventeenth century. He had a hand in the Rosicrucianism of his period and published some laws of the brotherhood, or alternatively those of an incorporated sodality based on similar lines. He was a man of great and exceptional learning, but withal of a fantastic spirit; he is proportionately difficult to judge, but his palmary concern was the material side of the *magnum opus*. He may have veered, and did probably, into other directions. The illustration is chosen from *The Golden Tripod*, being three ancient tracts attributed respectively to Basil Valentine, Thomas Norton, and John Cremer- a so-called abbot of Westminster. It is these personages who are apparently represented in the picture, together with the *zelator*, servant or pupil, attached to the master of the place, whose traditional duty was the maintenance with untiring zeal of the graduated fire of the art. Basil Valentine, in the course of his tract, makes it clear that he is concerned therein only with the physical work, and in the decorative manner which I have mentioned he affirms that if the three alchemical principles- namely, philosophical Mercury, Sulphur and Salt- can be rectified till "the metallic spirit and body are joined together inseparably by means of the metallic soul," the chain of love will he riveted firmly thereby and the palace prepared for the coronation.

But the substances in question are not those which are known under these names, and it is for this reason, or for reasons similar thereto, that no process of metallic alchemy can he followed practically by the isolated student, because everything essential is left out. The tradition is that the true key was imparted only from the adept to his son in the art. This notwithstanding, Basil Valentine calls the particular work to which I am here referring, The Twelve Keys, and it is said that they open the twelve doors leading to the Stone of the Philosophers and to the true Medicine. The same terminology would be used by the spiritual alchemists in another and higher sense; but this school possesses a master-key which opens all the doors. Basil Valentine's second key is that of Mercury, as it is pictured here below.

This, it will be seen, is the crowned or philosophical Mercury, bearing in either hand the caduceus, which is his characteristic emblem, and having wings upon his shoulders, signifying the volatilized state. But there are also wings beneath his feet, meaning that he has overcome this state, and has been fixed by the art of the sages, which is part of the Great Work, requiring the concurrence of the Sun and Moon, whose symbols appear behind him. The figures at either side carry on their wands or swords respectively the Bird of Hermes and a crowned serpent. The latter corresponds to that serpent which, by the command of Moses, was uplifted in the wilderness for the healing of the children of Israel. As in this figure Mercury has become a constant fire, one of the figures is shielding his face from the brilliance. He is on the side of the increasing moon, but on the side of the sun is he who has attained the Medicine, and he looks therefore with a steadfast face upon the unveiled countenance of the vision. According to Basil Valentine, Mercury is the principle of life. He says also that Saturn is the chief key of the art, though it is least useful in the mastery. The reference is to philosophical lead, and he gives a very curious picture representing this key, as it is shown on the next page [here below. Ed.].

The King in Basil Valentine's terminology is the stone
in its glorious rubefaction, or state of redness, when it
is surrounded by the whole court of the metals. The
Spouse of the King is Venus; Saturn is the Prefect of
the royal household; Jupiter is the Grand Marshal;
Mars is at the head of military affairs; Mercury has the
office of Chancellor; the Sun is Vice-Regent; the office
of the Moon is not named, but she seems to be a
Queen in widowhood. Before them there is borne the
banner attributed to each: that of the King is crimson,
emblazoned with the figure of Charity in green
garments; that of Saturn- which is carried by
Astronomy- is black, emblazoned with the figure of
Faith in garments of yellow and red; that of Jupiter-
which is carried by Rhetoric- is grey, emblazoned with

Hope in party-coloured garments; that of Mars is crimson, with Courage in a crimson cloak, and it is borne by Geometry; that of Mercury is carried by Arithmetic, and is a rainbow standard with the figure of Temperance, also in a many-coloured vestment; that of the Sun is a yellow banner, held by Grammar and exhibiting the figure of Justice in a golden robe; that of the Moon is resplendent silver, with the figure of Prudence, clothed in sky-blue, and it is borne by. Dialectic. Venus has no banner apart from that of the King, but her apparel is of gorgeous magnificence. I pass now to another order of symbolism which delineates the spiritual work by means of very curious pictures, accompanied by evasive letterpress. These are also from a Germanic source, and the writer-if not the designer-was Nicholas Barnaud, who went among many others in quest of Rosicrucians, but it does not appear what he found. I will give in the first place a Symbol which represents Putrefaction, being the disintegration of the rough matter in physical alchemy and on the spiritual side the mystery of mystical death. According to The Book of Lambspring, which is the name of the little treatise, the sages keep close guard over the secret of this operation, because the world is unworthy; and the children of philosophy, who receive its communication in part and carry it to the proper term by their personal efforts, enjoy it also in silence, since God wills that it should be hidden. This is the conquest of the dragon of material and manifest life; but it is like the old folklore fables, in which an act of violence is necessary to determine an enchantment for the redemption of those who are enchanted. The work is to destroy the body, that the body may not only be revived, but may live henceforth in a more perfect and as if incorruptible form. The thesis is that Nature is returned unto herself with a higher gift and more sacred warrant and the analogy among things familiar is the sanctification of intercourse by the sacrament of marriage. The dragon in this picture is destroyed by a knight, but we shall understand that he is clothed in the armour of God, and that St. Paul has described the harness.

The next illustration concerns the natural union between body soul and spirit; it is represented pictorially in the tract after more than one manner, as when two fishes are shown swimming in the sea, and it is said that the sea is the body. Here it is a stag and an unicorn, while the body is that forest which they range. The unicorn represents the spirit, and he who can couple them together and lead them out of the forest deserves to be called a Master, as the letterpress

The reason is that on their return to the body the flesh itself will he changed and will have been rendered golden. In respect of the alternative illustration, the mystery of this reunion is likened to a work of coaction, by which the three are so joined together that they are not afterwards sundered; and this signifies the Medicine. In yet another picture the spirit and soul are represented by a lion and lioness, between which an union must

must be effected before the work upon the body can be accomplished. It is an operation of great wisdom and even cunning, and he who performs it has merited the meed of praise before all others. I suppose that rough allegory could hardly express more plainly the marriage in the sanctified life between the human soul and the Divine Part. Neither text nor illustration continue so clear in the sequel, more especially as different symbols are used to represent the same things. In the next picture the war between the soul and the spirit is shown by that waged between a wolf and a dog, till one of them kills the other, and a poison is thus generated which restores them in some obscure manner, and they become the great and precious Medicine which in its turn restores the sages.

The tract then proceeds to the consideration of Mercury, and to all appearance has changed its subject, though this is not really the case, as might be demonstrated by an elaborate interpretation; but I omit this and the pictures thereto belonging, not only from considerations of space but because the task would be difficult, since it is not possible to say what the spiritual alchemists intended by Mercury, this being the secret of a particular school. When the sequence is again taken up the human trinity is presented under another veil, being that of the Father, the Son and the Guide. The symbolism is strangely confused, but some apologists would affirm that this was for a special purpose. In any case, the soul now appears as a boy; the Guide is the Spirit, and the illustration shows them at the moment of parting, when the soul is called to ascend, so that it may understand all wisdom and go even to the gate of Heaven. Their hands are interlinked, and it will he seen that the highest of all is distinguished- except for his wings- by an utter simplicity, characterized by his plain vestments. He, on the other hand, who represents

the body has the symbols of earthly royalty. The story concerning them tells how the Soul ascended till it beheld the throne of Heaven. The next picture is intended to set forth this vision, when the soul and spirit are seen on the high

mountain of initiation, with all the splendours of the
celestial canopy exhibited above them. It is said to be a
mountain in India, which in books of the Western
adepts seems always to have been regarded as the
symbolical soul's home and the land of epopts. The
text states, notwithstanding, that the mountain lies in
the vessel, and those who remember what was set forth
in my previous paper will know exactly what this
means- an intimation on the part of the alchemist that
lie is dealing only with events of experience belonging
to the world within. That which is expressed, however,
as a result of the vision is that the soul remembers the
body-spoken of here as the father- and longs to return
thereto, to which the Spirit Guide consents, and they
descend from that high eminence. Two things are
illustrated hereby- (1) that the soul in its progress
during incarnate life has the body to save and to
change, so that all things may be holy; but (2) that it is

possible- as is nearly always the case in parables of this kind- to offer a dual interpretation, and the alternative to that which I have given would be an allegory of return to the House of the Father in an entirely different sense. But it is obvious that I cannot speak of it- at least, in the present place. The next picture- and assuredly the most grotesque of all- represents the reunion of body and soul by the extraordinary

process of the one devouring the other, during which operation it should he noted that the spirit stands far apart. The text now approaches its close and delineates the construction of a reborn and glorified body, as the result of which it is said "The son ever remains in the father, and the father in the son... By the grace of God they abide for ever, the father and the son triumphing gloriously in the splendour of their new Kingdom." They sit upon one throne and between them is the spirit, the Ancient Master, who is arrayed in a crimson robe. So is the triadic union

accomplished, and herein is the spiritual understanding of that mystery which is called the Medicine in terms of alchemical philosophy. The finality of the whole subject can be expressed in a few words, and although it may be a dark saying for some of my readers it may prove a light to others, and for this reason I give it as follows: The experiment of spiritual alchemy was the Yoga process of the West. The root-reason of the statement must be already, as I think, obvious- probably from the present paper and assuredly from that which preceded it. The physical experiment of the magnum opus may have been carried in the past to a successful issue. I do not know, and of my concern it is no part; but those who took over the terminology of the transmutation of metals and carried it to another degree had opened gates within them which lead into the attainment of all desire in the order which is called absolute, because after its attainment all that we understand by the soul's dream has passed into the soul's reality. It is the dream of Divine Union, and eternity cannot exhaust the stages of its fulfillment.

www.ingramcontent.com/pod-product-compliance
Lightning Source LLC
Chambersburg PA
CBHW071753090426
42738CB00011B/2674